D1518687

History's Hotshots

SAMURAI!
Strong and Steady Warriors

Elsie Olson

Checkerboard
Library

An Imprint of Abdo Publishing
abdopublishing.com

abdopublishing.com

Published by Abdo Publishing, a division of ABDO, PO Box 398166, Minneapolis, Minnesota 55439.
Copyright © 2018 by Abdo Consulting Group, Inc. International copyrights reserved in all countries.
No part of this book may be reproduced in any form without written permission from the publisher.
Checkerboard Library™ is a trademark and logo of Abdo Publishing.

Printed in the United States of America, North Mankato, Minnesota
102017
012018

THIS BOOK CONTAINS
RECYCLED MATERIALS

Design: Kelly Doudna, Mighty Media, Inc.
Production: Mighty Media, Inc.
Editor: Jessie Alkire
Cover Photograph: Shutterstock
Design Elements: Shutterstock
Interior Photographs: Alamy, pp. 4-5, 8 (top), 8 (bottom), 10, 15, 21, 25; Cartoon Network/Alamy, p. 29;
iStockphoto, p. 7; Mighty Media, Inc., pp. 11, 23; Shutterstock, pp. 1, 11, 19, 23; Wikimedia Commons,
pp. 8 (middle), 9, 13, 17, 22, 27

Publisher's Cataloging-in-Publication Data

Names: Olson, Elsie, author.
Title: Samurai! strong and steady warriors / by Elsie Olson.
Other titles: Strong and steady warriors
Description: Minneapolis, Minnesota : Abdo Publishing, 2018. | Series: History's hotshots |
     Includes online resources and index.
Identifiers: LCCN 2017944052 | ISBN 9781532112744 (lib.bdg.) | ISBN 9781532150463 (ebook)
Subjects: LCSH: Samurai--Juvenile literature. | Samurai--History--Juvenile literature. |
     Japan--History, Military--To 1868--Juvenile literature. | Japan--Juvenile literature.
Classification: DDC 952.02508--dc23
LC record available at https://lccn.loc.gov/2017944052

Contents

The BATTLE BEGINS

It's the morning of a great battle. You are dressed in your finest armor. An **intricate** helmet protects your head. Scaled metal plates protect your chest and thighs. Two swords hang at your side. Your bow is at the ready, arrows strapped to your back.

You wait on your faithful horse, side by side with the other samurai who serve your shogun. If you are afraid, you don't show it. In fact, you have been trained to not show fear. And you have been preparing for such a battle since you were only three years old. This is what you were born to do.

Your fellow warriors also show no fear. Like you, they follow a strict code of loyalty and honor. They have pledged to give their lives for their shogun if required. You hope today's battle will end in victory or death. There is no room for defeat. You hear your commander give the call to fight, and you urge your horse forward as the battle begins. You are part of the highest class in Japanese society. You are a samurai warrior!

CHAPTER 1

Who Were the Samurai?

The samurai were members of the **elite** Japanese warrior class. They came to power in Japan in the 1100s. They remained active until the mid-1800s. Samurai played an important role in Japan's history. In fact, they ruled the country for hundreds of years through a military **dictator** called a shogun.

Being a samurai was a lifetime commitment. It was also a great honor. Most samurai warriors were born into samurai families. Only men could be samurai. They were trained from a very young age. They became experts in **martial arts** and swordsmanship.

The samurai followed a strict code of honor. Samurai valued loyalty above all else. Lower samurai served daimyos, or land-owning lords. The daimyos served the shogun and his family. All were members of the samurai class. Samurai would fight and die to defend their leader's honor. A samurai would rather die than lose a battle.

While the samurai were fierce fighters, they were also accomplished off the battlefield. When they weren't fighting

Samurai were expected to be extremely serious. They also valued kindness, honesty, and morals.

or training, samurai were known to write poetry, paint, and arrange flowers. Most practiced **Buddhism**.

Timeline

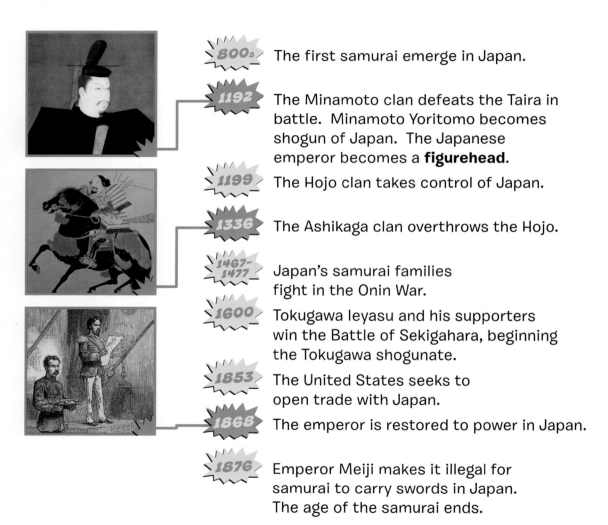

800s — The first samurai emerge in Japan.

1192 — The Minamoto clan defeats the Taira in battle. Minamoto Yoritomo becomes shogun of Japan. The Japanese emperor becomes a **figurehead**.

1199 — The Hojo clan takes control of Japan.

1336 — The Ashikaga clan overthrows the Hojo.

1467–1477 — Japan's samurai families fight in the Onin War.

1600 — Tokugawa Ieyasu and his supporters win the Battle of Sekigahara, beginning the Tokugawa shogunate.

1853 — The United States seeks to open trade with Japan.

1868 — The emperor is restored to power in Japan.

1876 — Emperor Meiji makes it illegal for samurai to carry swords in Japan. The age of the samurai ends.

Tokugawa Ieyasu

Tokugawa Ieyasu started the most powerful samurai **dynasty** in Japanese history. He was born in 1543 in Okazaki, Japan. His father was a lord until his death in 1549. In 1547, Tokugawa was held captive by a rival clan. He was released in 1560 and returned to his family castle. Tokugawa formed **alliances** with other lords and began fighting for more control of Japan. But the lords soon turned against one another, and war broke out.

In 1600, Tokugawa won the Battle of Sekigahara. This victory left Tokugawa as Japan's only shogun. In 1605, he retired, passing the shogunate to his son Tokugawa Hidetada. Tokugawa Ieyasu remained involved in the leadership of the shogunate until his death in 1616. And the Tokugawa clan controlled Japan for the next two centuries.

CHAPTER 2

Birth of the Samurai

For much of Japan's history, the islands were divided into clans. Clans competed against one another for land and resources. But by 400, Japan was united under one emperor. Wealthy landowners were scattered throughout the country. They were ruled by the emperor in the capital of Kyoto. The first samurai emerged in the 800s. These were warriors who fought for wealthy landowners.

Eventually, certain samurai families became powerful on their own. These families controlled certain areas of Japan. Two samurai families, the Taira and Minamoto clans, became especially powerful. They fought one another for more than 100 years. Then, in 1192, the Minamoto clan defeated the Taira.

During his rule, Minamoto Yoritomo declared that no one could call himself a samurai without Minamoto's permission.

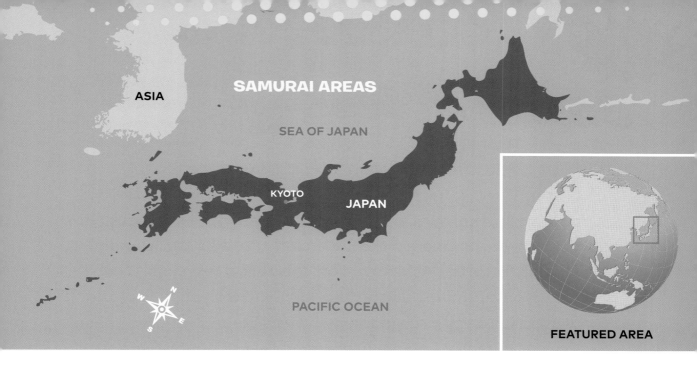

The emperor made samurai leader Minamoto Yoritomo the shogun of Japan. But Minamoto took away the emperor's power. Minamoto now controlled Japan. The emperor became a **figurehead**. In fact, Japanese emperors would be nearly powerless for the next 700 years. The era of samurai rule had begun.

Minamoto died in 1199. His wife's family, the Hojo clan, took over control of Japan. They ruled the country for the next 100 years. They fought off other clans seeking to overthrow them. But in 1274, the family faced a new threat from afar.

CHAPTER 3

Japan at War

In the 1200s, **Mongols** were invading Asia and Eastern Europe. In 1274 and 1281, the Mongols attempted to invade Japan. The samurai managed to fight off both attacks. But the attacks weakened the Hojo clan's hold on the islands.

In 1336, the Ashikaga clan overthrew the Hojo. The Ashikaga clan ruled Japan for the next 200 years. But they were constantly challenged by other samurai families. Then, from 1467 to 1477, the country was divided by the Onin War. During this time, other powerful families fought the Ashikaga clan for control. By the end of the war, Kyoto was in ruins. Japan was left largely leaderless.

For the next 150 years, the islands were in a state of almost constant conflict. This era is known as the Age of Warring States. During this time, Japan was divided into many samurai families led by daimyos. These daimyos fought one another over power. It was also a time of great military advancement. The samurai

Hotshot Fact

New weapons, such as exploding arrows and fire spears, were used during the Onin War.

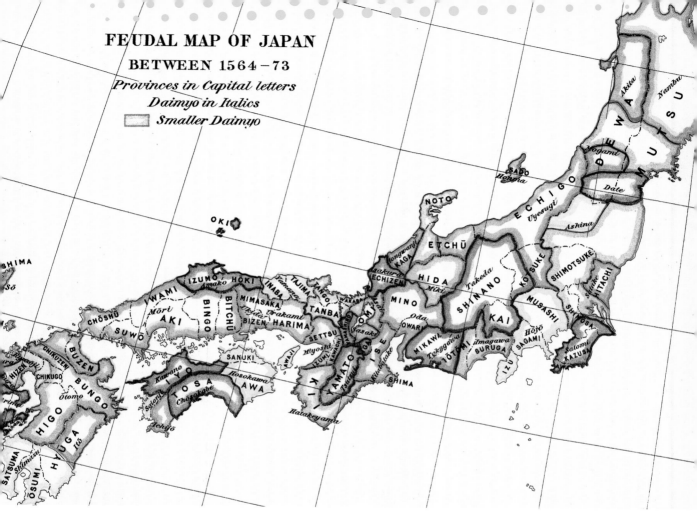

FEUDAL MAP OF JAPAN
BETWEEN 1564–73
Provinces in Capital letters
Daimyo in Italics
☐ **Smaller Daimyo**

Daimyos made their own laws and often operated on their own, without much shogun control.

looked for new weapons and fighting methods to use against enemies.

CHAPTER 4

End of the Samurai Age

In 1591, samurai Toyotomi Hideyoshi managed to gain control of a united Japan. But his reign was short-lived. Toyotomi died in 1598, leaving his power to his son Hideyori. In 1600, daimyo Tokugawa Ieyasu challenged Hideyori. Tokugawa won the Battle of Sekigahara and became shogun of Japan.

Tokugawa and his descendants ruled Japan for the next 250 years. During his reign, Tokugawa set up new laws to maintain control of Japan. He limited trade with other countries. Tokugawa's descendants made it illegal for anyone who wasn't a samurai to carry a sword. Daimyos' families were kept as **hostages** in the capital.

In 1853, the United States wanted to open trade with the islands. Japan was divided over whether or not to trade with the United States. The conflict led to the Tokugawa clan being overthrown. In the 1860s, young samurai fought to restore power to the emperor. They were successful. In 1868, Emperor Meiji was made ruler of Japan.

Meiji took steps to make sure samurai would not challenge his authority. In 1876, he made it illegal to carry

In 1889, Emperor Meiji proclaimed the Meiji Constitution. This set of government rules was presented as a gift from the emperor to the people.

samurai swords. He also built a national military. The samurai would always hold an important place in Japanese history and **culture**. But the age of samurai rule was over.

CHAPTER 5

Becoming a Samurai

Samurai were born into the warrior class. This was the highest class in Japanese society. During the Tokugawa rule, up to ten percent of Japan's population may have been members of the samurai class. Samurai were highly respected. Members of other classes were required to bow when samurai walked past!

Samurai began training from a very young age. Boys who belonged to poorer samurai families were often trained by older family members, such as fathers, brothers, or uncles. Some boys from wealthy families were sent to academies to train with samurai masters. The students learned **martial arts**, military skills, swordplay, and more. They also studied **Buddhism**, poetry, **calligraphy**, and other arts.

Whether it took place at home or at an academy, samurai training was very demanding. Boys began learning how to use a sword at as young as three years old! By age five, they began learning martial arts. Some samurai masters hit their students when they weren't expecting it. This prepared the students to be ready for an attack at all times.

Samurai used wooden weapons against one another while training. They used metal weapons to practice fighting on wooden or straw dummies.

Life as a Samurai

While all samurai were trained as fighters, they spent much of their time off the battlefield. Samurai usually divided their time between their daimyo's castle and their own lands. In addition to managing their estates, samurai read and wrote poetry, painted, played games, and practiced **Buddhism**.

Samurai often gained profits from their estates, usually through farming. They were also given a **stipend** for their service as samurai. At the time, Japanese currency was measured in a year's supply of rice, called a koku. Depending on how high a samurai's status was, he might receive from one to more than 100 koku per year!

WOMEN OF THE SAMURAI AGE

While the word *samurai* only applied to men, Japanese women of this period were also fierce fighters. Many women were trained in **martial arts** from a young age. They carried knives and weren't afraid to use them. Higher-status women also learned how to fight with short swords called *naginatas*.

The former home of the Nomura, a samurai family in Kanazawa, Japan, is open to the public. It has decorative ceilings, paintings, and a garden with a waterfall!

Samurai wives were expected to use these weapons to defend their homes and families if attacked. Wives also managed the finances of their husbands' estates.

CHAPTER 7

Way of the Warrior

Samurai followed a strict code of conduct known as **Bushido,** or "the way of the warrior." This was not a written set of rules. Instead, it was a set of values samurai were expected to hold. The samurai code valued courage, honor, and loyalty. Samurai were expected to fight to the death to defend their lords and their honor.

Death was a way of life for a samurai. He was expected to think about and prepare for his death every day. If a samurai risked losing a battle or somehow dishonored his lord, he was expected to commit seppuku. In this act, the samurai would take his own life by stabbing himself in the stomach.

Samurai were also expected to commit seppuku upon the deaths of their masters. Those who chose not to were known as ronin. Sometimes ronin fought to avenge their masters' deaths. More often, they became paid fighters or thieves. Such ronin gave other ronin a bad reputation among samurai.

Samurai often committed seppuku in a ceremony. The samurai would drink sake, a Japanese rice wine, and write a death poem before the act.

Samurai Appearance

Part of the samurai warrior code was setting a good example for the lower classes. Samurai dressed with great care. A samurai typically wore an undergarment called a kimono. Over the kimono, he would wear loose pants and a loose jacket. A belt called an obi held the samurai's swords.

A samurai also took great care with his hair. Most samurai kept their hair long and pulled back in a bun. But samurai often wore their hair down during battle.

Samurai armor changed over time. But the armor most people associate with samurai is the *o-yoroi*. Samurai wore this armor in the 1100s and 1200s. It was lightweight and made of metal scales that were bound together

Samurai also paid attention to their horses' appearance. They dressed the animals in armor, masks, and other decorative items.

KUWAGATA
(STAGBEETLE ANTENNAE)

FUKIKAESSHI
(NECK GUARD)

KABUTO-NO-A
(CHIN STRAP)

SENDAN-NO-ITA
(BREAST PLATE)

OOSODA
(SHOULDER
GUARD)

OBI
(BELT)

KUSAZURI
(THIGH GUARD)

TSURANUKI
(LEATHER SHOES)

into plates. The plates were then coated in **lacquer**, which made them **waterproof**. The armor protected the wearer from attacks by bow and arrow.

A helmet protected the samurai's head from arrows and sword blows. It was made of metal and included cheek guards. The helmet had a hole in the top where the samurai's bun could stick out.

CHAPTER 9

Samurai Weapons

Samurai fought with many different weapons. Early samurai used bows and arrows to attack their enemies from horseback. Spears were also favored by samurai. Samurai spears were known as *yari*. The yari featured a double-edged blade attached to a long wooden shaft.

The most famous samurai weapon was the sword. Samurai carried two swords, a short sword called a *wakizashi* and a long sword called a katana. The katana was most used during battle. This sword was crafted from steel and had a curved blade. It was lightweight but sharp enough to cut through bone. The katana could also act as a shield and **deflect** a blow from another sword. Katanas were highly valued and passed down through families for generations.

In 1510, guns were brought to Japan from China. Japanese gun makers soon began producing their own weapons. These weapons became common in battles. However, many samurai viewed guns

Hotshot Fact

Samurai boys who were born left-handed were trained to use their right hands. As a result, very few samurai fought left-handed.

A samurai could draw his sword and strike his victim in a single motion.

as inferior to traditional weapons because they took less skill to operate.

CHAPTER 10

Samurai in Battle

When a daimyo issued a call to arms, the samurai were quick to answer. They fought on horseback or on foot. Samurai used many different weapons in the same battle. They might begin with bow and arrow, then switch to swords, and finish fighting by hand.

Samurai armor provided good protection from katana and arrows. So, attackers aimed for a samurai's weak spots, such as the face, which wasn't always covered in armor. Attackers would also try to hit an opponent many times.

Samurai wore small markers called *sashimono* on their backs. These helped identify which daimyo they fought for. Samurai were famous for taking their opponents' heads as battle trophies. This proved they had been victorious in battle. The heads would be cleaned and groomed. Samurai would then present the heads to their daimyos.

Hotshot Fact

Occasionally, samurai would put their enemies under siege. They would surround an enemy city, withholding its resources. However, most daimyo preferred active battle.

鹿児島城

Samurai battles followed common practices. Samurai would ride out on horseback and call out their achievements and ancestry to find a suitable opponent.

Samurai Today

The role of the samurai warrior in Japan declined quickly in the late 1800s. Daimyos lost their power when **feudalism** was officially abolished in 1871. Modern Japan no longer has a samurai class. However, samurai still hold an important place in modern Japanese culture.

The values maintained by the samurai code, including loyalty and honor, are still highly valued in Japanese society. **Martial arts** are still practiced in Japan. Other sports teams, including baseball and soccer, also reference the way of the warrior. Coaches and players value aspects of the samurai code, including fairness, determination, and hard work.

Samurai continue to fascinate many other cultures as well. Samurai movies are popular with viewers all over the globe. Many of these films are in Japanese. Others, such as 2003's *The Last Samurai*, are in English.

In 2001, Cartoon Network began airing a cartoon called *Samurai Jack* in the United States. The show focuses on a young samurai who is sent into the future and must defeat a shape-shifting enemy named Aku. *Samurai Jack* ran

Most episodes of Samurai Jack focus on obstacles Jack must overcome to find his way back home and defeat his enemy. However, Jack usually loses his chance and must continue his quest.

until 2004. In 2017, the show was revived for one season. While the age of samurai may have ended, these warriors are far from forgotten!

Glossary

alliance – a group of people or nations united for some special purpose.

Buddhism – a religion of eastern and central Asia based on the teachings of Gautama Buddha.

Bushido – the code of conduct developed by samurai.

calligraphy – decorative handwriting or handwritten lettering.

culture – the customs, arts, and tools of a nation or a people at a certain time.

deflect – to turn something aside from a fixed or straight path.

dictator – a ruler with complete control who often governs in a cruel or unfair way.

dynasty – a series of rulers who belong to the same family.

elite – of or relating to the best of a class.

feudalism – a social system in which people served lords. In return, people received the lord's protection and use of land.

figurehead – a leader with an important title who exercises little real power.

hostage – a person captured by another person or group in order to make a deal with authorities.

intricate – having parts that are arranged in a complex or elaborate manner.

lacquer – a liquid that is spread on wood or metal and dries to form a hard and shiny surface.

martial arts – an art of combat or self-defense practiced as a sport.

Mongols – a group of nomadic people from Mongolia.

stipend – a fixed regular sum paid as a salary or allowance.

waterproof – not allowing water to pass through.

Online Resources

Booklinks NONFICTION NETWORK
FREE! ONLINE NONFICTION RESOURCES

To learn more about samurai, visit abdobooklinks.com. These links are routinely monitored and updated to provide the most current information available.

Index